6/24

The Art of Presence

One Path Toward Peace

Joanne O'Neil

To my two shining beings, Kira and Jesse

INTRODUCTION

THE BONES OF THIS SMALL BOOK WERE WRITTEN IN 1997 as part of a larger work written for my master's thesis. At that time, the idea of presence as a clear and essential aspect of any therapeutic or healing relationship did not seem well known. I attempted to translate the various tangents on the subject and make it more accessible to the general public. My vision was then—and is still today—to illuminate the gorgeous simplicity of the art of being fully present to another person. The practice of presence is integral to health in all forms: mental and emotional, spiritual, of interpersonal relationships, of communities, and even of the world.

Webster's Dictionary defines "present" as a state of being "self possessed, collected, ready."[1] The *Concise Oxford Dictionary* declares that "presence (of mind) is calmness and self-command in sudden emergencies." In this book I endeavor to convey more about these concepts and to assist the reader to develop a fuller appreciation of the way of being named "presence" and what it can offer when practiced. The practice of presence can help us learn to live more fully in each moment and stay connected to our authentic, inner selves while managing the complex, everyday world around us.

It seems to me that the crisis of this century is a crisis of faith. We are being called to cultivate deep integrity in the way we conduct ourselves, connecting to others in a non-judgmental attitude of equanimity and tender-hearted truthfulness. The adventurous stream of consciousness that exists within all art forms must be brought back into our everyday lives, as intrinsic aspects of our communities, and embraced as essential components for the vibrant health of our children and our humanity. We are going to need extraordinary imagination to fare well and creatively in the future and to maintain a vision of a world that is a healed, whole, and supportive environment for life. We must value peace in our own hearts first if we desire it to grow in the larger world. Practicing presence is one path toward discovering that peace.

During the past twenty years many have written about mindfulness, meditation, and presence. These writers include our many extraordinary contemporary Buddhist teachers, among them the His Holiness the fourteenth Dalai Lama, Thich Nhat Hanh, Pema Chodren, and Jack Kornfield. Many more individuals have contributed to the teachings and practices of meditation, mindfulness, and the contemplative arts. These include Jon Kabat-Zinn, John Welwood, Frances Vaughn, Ken Wilbur, Marc Epstein, Jean Houston, and Joan Borysenko, among numerous others. My twenty-two years of studies with extraordinary herbal teachers and leaders has added another layer of depth to my personal understanding of presence and mindfulness. Herbal teachers and writers including Kate Gilday, Stephen Buhner, Matthew Wood, Deb Soule, Amanda McQuade Crawford, Christopher Hobbs, Rosemary Gladstar, David Winston, Pam Montgomery, Margi Flint, and Eliot Cowan. They teach the science of the extensive world of medicinal plants, including their identification, habitat, signature, and medicinal preparations. They also teach about the rich, expansive world of knowledge available to those who practice presence and conscious mindfulness while working directly with plants. This is a way of being present in the natural world—focused, open, aware, and awake to nuances and subtleties.

The plant world echoes our richly patterned, interwoven human coexistence. Learning to be present in the natural world with respect, curiosity, and openness invites a different way of interacting with one another as humans. This metaphysical journey, full of complex information, nurtures and enlivens our sense of interconnectedness with all living beings. Practicing presence in the natural world is a direct way into discovering the natural rhythms and flow of life.

To reconnect with the natural world on a consistent basis today is to renew and refresh the ties that bind us as living beings. Practicing presence in the natural world promotes a sense of ease and well-being while reminding us of our profound global interdependence. It is a missing aspect in many healing modalities currently employed for the treatment of depression, anxiety, and disease. I humbly invite us to reconsider the natural world as a component intrinsically related to all essential wellness care.

I believe that this art of learning to be fully present in one's own life, and subsequently in all relationships, is first facilitated by practicing meditation and cultivating peace within. I studied spiritual psychology, as taught by Tom Yeomans at the Concord Institute, over a period of eight years. In each configuration of students and trainings, we practiced the Guidelines for Group Dialogue. These guidelines serve as a profound core approach to practicing presence. They include active and deep listening, learning to bear intensity, suspending blame or judgment while listening to the truth of another's experience, slowing down, breathing, embracing silence, welcoming the unknown, and demonstrating patience. Consistent practice of these guidelines yields authentic, meaningful, and, eventually, graceful and honest communication. Practicing presence reminds us of our innate wisdom and natural humanness. My ongoing personal practice of meditation and conscious application of these guidelines have increased my capacity for kindness, compassion, and listening skills in my personal and professional life.

All relationships, including those with ourself, can expand and improve when we become awake and present to their deeper aspects. The ideas I propose in this book are not only for trained authorities, but for all of us to be able to learn and practice in everyday life. My ongoing contemplative practices inform my practice of presence and seem to invite a spaciousness and depth to emerge in many forums. This is particularly noticeable in my therapy practice with clients, but it also creates room for new patience, the ability to listen to the other side of a disagreement, and openness to new experiences.

Our natural state is open, relaxed, and aware, yet our contemporary life seems to get in the way of that state of being. Often, I hear that it feels like a lot of work to be relaxed and open, and people do not always remember how or when that happened in their lives. Practicing presence is one path toward revitalizing that natural state of being.

The practice of meditation and contemplative practices, the cultivation of stillness and silence within, and more time spent in the natural world inform and enlighten the practice of presence. Each of these creates room for new patience and an increased ability to listen well. This, in turn, invites us to be open to new ideas and experiences. It also cultivates open-heartedness.

Developing the capacity to be fully present takes practice and patience, particularly with ourselves. Learning to be present to the truth of one's own experience is a preparation for getting in touch with our deeper nature. Living fully infers embracing both the joys and difficulties of one's life. I believe that if we could all practice moments of presence with each other on a consistent basis, we might begin to discover the possibility that we are all spiritual beings having a human experience. This is not my original idea, but it is one that resonates for many. The idea could transform the way we think and treat each other as we stumble along our way toward peace.

Presence is a conscious appreciation of one another. Learning to be fully present is a practice, indeed an art, like no other. It requires us to be still and listen, really listen. As we give another person our full attention, the energetic space between us pulsates and surrounds us as if a container is being built. This container is infused with an essence of *something more*. In these moments, small shifts in consciousness can occur. They can seem relatively inconsequential in the moment, but those initial shifts create openings in perspective that linger and expand.

There are many paths to presence, to the rediscovery of our connection to a deeper place within. Foundations for creating a healthy, meaningful, and conscious life include spending time in the natural world, mindfulness meditation, breathing exercises, movement and relaxation exercises, finding meaningful connections in our community, and compassionate self-care. They are also initiatory steps on a journey back to ourselves, our core, and our rich, inner soulfulness. My deepest desire is that some part of this book will touch you, spark your imagination, or assist you in regaining something precious and valuable that you had lost or forgotten.

Embrace the complexity.

Sit with the mystery.

Become open to what is hidden.

Discover connections in the truth.

Breathe. Let go of fear.

Invite aliveness back into your life.

Acknowledgments

Many of my comrades supported this project. I am grateful to Susan Murphy for lending the use of her beautiful art gracing the cover. To Ed Ritz for believing in me; his generous support and encouragement helped to bring this book into the world. To Michelle Gabow, who told me to trust my instincts and gave me confidence to add my voice to the larger world. And to my circle of abiding friends and family, intelligentsia all, whose encouragement along the way provided a lightness of being to the lonelier stretches of research and writing—for all the delightful meals, laughter, levity, stories, and songs—among them: Susan and Ed, Ingrid Wilgren, Diane Rossman, Michele LaCroix, Maureen O'Neil, Hugh Hall, Zachary O'Neil, Nick O'Neil, Kate Gilday, Don Babineau, Chris Morano, Lindsay Norris, Julia LeGrant, Liz Granfort, Lillian Miranda, Bob, Holly, and George Ghazey, Carol Drexler, Penny Gill, and Anna Greene.

I am indebted to my Spiritual Psychology Community of Practice, a true dharma community unlike any other, and one for whom practicing presence became a living art. Many passionate conversations and long hours and days sitting together in our circle, practicing the guidelines, and discovering the true beauty of the process with time and patience, have indelibly etched the vital aspects and gifts of the practice of presence in my mind and heart. You each live in my heart.

I am deeply thankful to Tom Yeomans, my teacher, mentor, and colleague. Your enduring reflections on the importance of presence and the depth and breadth of your teachings on the many aspects and forms of presence offered significant guidance and inspiration. Your leadership and modeling of presence in all respects made it breathe and come alive so that now there is no other way.

I thank my editor Jean Zimmer for keeping me focused, being patient with my process, gently reminding me of the unique realities of a writer's life, and for keeping my tenses straight and my writing clear. You were a pleasure to work with, Jean. To Steve Strimer and the Collective Copies folks for creating the book as I saw it in my mind's eye, thanks!

I offer thanks and a rich appreciation to my mother, Peggy O'Neil, who listens so well and without judgment, and who has always believed in me, a true gift. And to my father, John O'Neil, greatly missed, for his unvarnished love and insisting that I be able to quote my sources in discussions. That lesson in my teens taught me so much!

Finally, I extend gratitude beyond words to my enchanting children, Kira and Jesse O'Neil Bona, for never losing faith in me and continuing the conversations, wherever they lead, with graceful intelligence, patience, loving kindness, and easy receipt of my endless explorations beyond the boundaries of conventional thought. You have made this life adventure ever so wonderful.

Table of Contents

CHAPTER ONE

OUR NATURAL STATE IS OPEN, RELAXED, AND AWARE. In this state we are fully present, to ourselves and to others. Yet this state of presence has become an art to practice in our contemporary lives of technological expertise and multitasking. Rediscovering this natural and authentic state of attention and awareness is an essential tool for increased peace of mind. Practicing presence promotes ease in communication. Presence is easy to cultivate and practice and has positive effects in all of our interactions and connections with others.

Presence is a central aspect of human psychological health and maturity. Presence teaches us to respond rather than to react. The practice of presence instructs us in the ability not to be drawn into distractions, reactions, projections, or defenses. Cultivating presence is a way of bearing witness, not only to others and the larger world, but also to ourselves.

Practicing Presence

Rest in your breathing.
Let go of having to say anything.
Let go of having to rescue or fix anyone.
Welcome the other with loving non-judgment.
Continue to rest while being highly active.

– Tom Yeomans

Defining the Art of Presence

Practicing presence opens a doorway for
deeper connection and relatedness.

Presence enables us to rediscover the art of truly listening. When we are fully present to another being, we are completely undistracted by our own inner voices, inner turmoil, or personal agenda. Presence encourages the cultivation of perspective. It supports our natural inner stirring toward wholeness and maturity.

The *art* of presence invites a non-judgmental attitude of re- ceptiveness. This creates an open approach and promotes the cultivation of perspective. Practicing presence allows us to learn to trust in our own experience, from moment to moment. As we practice being open and nonjudgmental toward others for short but concentrated periods of time, we become more prepared to offer that perspective with others, more often. Ultimately, the practice of presence is about learning to sit with the unknown, the mystery—in relation to others. Through presence, communi- cation is clarified; presence fosters openness and genuine dis- course, which can transform relationships. The practices of meditation and mindfulness can deepen the art of presence. The art of presence involves opening to our ever-present awareness to our radiant, open, compassionate, resilient, and fundamen- tally authentic self.

Presence invites a more conscious appreciation of one an- other. Responsiveness grows as reactivity diminishes. Trust the process. Slow down. Relax. Breathe.

As we practice being with another person without judgment, letting go of preconceived notions or ideas about that person or what we expect to be said, a different level of integrity naturally occurs. Listening fully, while transcending our own inner thought processes with an expansive attitude, invites the possibility for new information and a fresh experience. Often, a resonance will emerge that surprises and enriches our mutual understanding.

My lifetime listens to yours.

– Muriel Rukeyser

Being fully present to one another takes both practice and patience at first. Most of us are not used to practicing the art of active listening. The experience of fully listening, without speaking back, simply being completely engaged in paying attention to—or being with—another person without interruptions, is less than usual in our modern, fast-paced, highly technological society. Therefore, it may feel a bit unfamiliar when we begin to actually pay close attention without distractions. Presence is a way to connect more deeply with people we are already close to and a way to invite a larger awareness of those who we would like to know and understand better.

 ### Exercise 1 – Practicing presence

Sit face-to-face in a quiet, comfortable place with a family member or close friend. Set a timer for five minutes. Let one person speak and the other only listen. Talk about anything of interest. Allow silence to enter naturally. Do not force words during those silent moments when they occur. Speak calmly and truthfully, without hiding emotions, trying not to self-judge while you are speaking.

When the timer sounds, *without conversation*, set it again for five minutes, and switch roles. The other person speaks and the first person listens. After the exercise, spend a few minutes sharing how this experience felt.

Practicing presence is very respectful. It is also relaxing. It generates a process for layers of the truth of experience to unfold. The stillness and quiet within the process itself creates a spaciousness for *something more* to happen. Listening fully, without judgment, is a gift to both the person listening with presence and the person being heard. It *feels* different to be listened to closely. Something ineffable shifts in our relationship to the words and ideas we speak, even as we hear ourselves speak them.

Simplicity is completely absorbed
in listening to what it hears.

– Thomas Merton

Developing the capacity to be fully present is indeed an art. We each have the capacity and aptitude to acquire it. Living fully infers embracing both the joys and difficulties of one's life. When we practice presence, we increase our ability to bear the intensities of our complex and complicated contemporary existence. We become more capable of a *both/and* perspective. This capacity to "hold both" means we stay centered while holding/recognizing duality and polarities. We might discover that we are able to notice a gorgeous sunset while still grieving. We become capable of sitting quietly with a child reading a bedtime story while also feeling deep sadness. We can listen well while still angry or hurt about a previous interaction and allow new information to assist us in moving forward. We can forgive even if we do not forget. Cultivating a both/and perspective is a spiritually mature perspective. Practicing presence can initiate this growth.

4

Presence encourages the cultivation of perspective. It supports our natural inner stirring toward wholeness and maturity. As we begin to trust in the truth of our own experience, from moment to moment, we slowly begin to notice nuances and details of our experiences. From an emotional and psychological perspective, the practice of presence cultivates a center within us from which we are able to be aware of the contents of our personal experience without being overly identified with those contents. Presence and mindful attention allow us a place to rest in our own truth, to discover our own inner stillness—and then to respond rather than react.

We sat alone in a small room off to the side with a few tables and some chairs. The windows, set high up in the wall, allowed a weak light into the space. He sat with his head in his hands, sobbing, his shoulders shaking. His face was ravaged from the previous few days, and he appeared older than his years. The last few months, years perhaps, had taken their toll on his youth and seeming nonchalance. My heart ached for his despair, his deep sorrow, and I spread my love around him like a blanket. I sat quietly next to him.

His sobbing gentled, but he kept his head bowed, weeping quietly now. "I feel as if I am losing my life," he said. I put my hand softly on his back, over his heart, leaning into his grief alongside him, saying nothing. We sat for a long time like this. When he finally raised his tear-streaked face to mine, I gently touched his arm, my face telling him everything he needed to know. It would be a long journey, but it had begun.

Ring the bells that can still ring.
Forget your perfect offering.
There is a crack in everything.
That's how the light gets in.

– Leonard Cohen[2]

Spiritual psychology theory suggests that the greater the degree of mystery or unknown that we can tolerate, the greater our emotional and psychological growth. Letting go of the need to know creates space for an evolution of thoughts and ideas. This spaciousness allows room for fixed ideas to shift, and sometimes to fall away. We become more supple in our thinking. When we allow ourselves to move toward the unknown, closer to mystery, our sense of wonder, curiosity, and aliveness increases.

It is said that spiritual growth is not about the self at all. The real work begins when we step out of the spotlight (of our own inner universe) and begin to define ourselves within a larger framework of meaning. This "meaning" can have many names, take many forms. Ultimately, a broader perspective and openness to others' ideas and viewpoints invites a more comprehensive interpretation of the world as a prismatic, expansive experience rather than a monocular, contractive vision.

When are fully present, we invite the unknown. Letting go of the need to know, or to be right, or imagining that we already *do* know or understand everything about another person creates the freedom to see the complexity and depth inherent in our experience of life. This way of being present with one another is an invitation to express ourselves truthfully and fearlessly.

Tolerating a degree of mystery makes space for a novel idea, an innovative thought process, and an openness to new information. The state of consciousness that emerges is often non-conceptual. Many people refer to a sense of heightened alertness, without tension. In this relaxed alertness, transformative reflections begin to enter our conscious thought field. This ability to practice presence, to bear the intensity of a situation and the thinking patterns of another being, facilitates movement and growth in our own lives as well. We learn the truth not only through our reasoning but also through our heart. The keys to being present are quieting within, actively listening, and focusing. Open-heartedness often follows.

Practicing listening to others with a "beginner's mind" invites an unsullied view to be considered. When we allow a curiousness and openness with another, a softening occurs. There is a rich complexity in each of us. Being fully present, living completely in the here and now, even for a short while, increases the capacity to be in touch with the truth of one's own, and others', present experience. Living in the present moment leads us to full contact with others and an innate recognition of our kinship.

> *Practicing presence helps to cultivate an inner centeredness, which gives us perspective and freedom from overreactions, defenses, and impulses, so that we are less likely to react unconsciously as conditions change around us. Rather, we get to choose, on the basis of our wisdom and calm understanding, the best course to take.*[3]

Practicing presence is surprisingly simple yet richly complex. The process is inherent in each of us and taps into subliminal knowing and buried wisdom. Our brains and physical beings (the body/mind/spirit continuum) know far more than what is normally available to us in an ordinary state of consciousness. It seems that we are conscious of merely fragments of what we know deep within. Our body's central nervous system perceives and processes a great body of information that is usually stored outside the range of our everyday awareness. Certainly, some of this information is best handled on an unconscious basis. Yet conflict and unresolved issues can become the source of chronic uneasiness, depression, or blocked creative expression.

Learning to pay close attention to the multifaceted knowledge contained within the body/mind/spirit continuum we call being human can move us into a rich and sometimes unexpected territory of personal insight and creative potential. The possibility of a fully experienced participation in one's own life is deeply connected to our clarity and inner vision. We can learn ways to access that clarity, our natural instincts, and our intuitive nature with the practice of presence. Meditation and the cultivation of mindfulness are the tools.

CHAPTER TWO

Cultivating Mindfulness

Mindfulness practice ... does not have specific goals, but is
open-ended. It could easily be practiced for a lifetime,
for broadening and deepening awareness has no limit.

— John Welwood[4]

MINDFULNESS ASSISTS US IN EXPERIENCING increased well-being by focusing our awareness, or "wise attention," and attunement to the present moment. It is our innate capacity to purposefully pay attention in a non-judging way. This idea is deeply rooted in most cultures, religions, and wisdom traditions worldwide. The foundation of mindfulness practice is to directly participate in each moment as it occurs, with as much awareness as possible. Genuine awareness is liberating and clarifying. Practices that intentionally focus awareness in the present moment are known to assist in transforming people's lives.

The simple act of sitting quietly and paying attention to the breath moving in and out of our bodies creates an awareness that heightens the senses, expands our perceptual realities, and nurtures our sense of inner peace. This mindful breathing is a powerful means of developing concentration.

Jon Kabat-Zinn, professor of medicine and founding director of the Stress Reduction Clinic and the Center for Mindfulness in Medicine, Health Care, and Society at the University of Massachusetts Medical School, teaches mindfulness meditation as a technique to help people cope with stress, anxiety, pain, and illness. He states that mindfulness, a particular kind of awareness, is cultivated by paying attention. We develop and refine this particular form of paying attention through the practice of mindfulness meditation, focusing techniques, and contemplative practice.

The mindfulness necessary to prepare, train, and perform a skill expertly arises beyond the thinking mind. Mastery in any field of endeavor implies that the thinking mind is out of the way for the moment. Mindfulness involves the self-regulation of attention. Artistic creation, meditation, yoga, breath work, tai chi, chanting, singing, playing musical instruments, drumming, dancing, theater, martial arts, teaching, counseling, playing sports, ritual, and ceremony—each, practiced and done well, creates an expanded awareness. These activities lead us into mindful awareness states that enhance physical, mental, emotional, spiritual, and social well-being. The awareness that emerges is open, expansive, and rich. This type of mastery is beyond control. Another kind of "intelligence" takes precedence. It is difficult to think about the problems from the workday when you are trying to follow your yoga teacher's guidance to practice a new yoga position as smoothly as possible!

Practicing any activity with mindful attention reveals small, transformational moments of peaceful presence and inner stillness. Rocking a baby, washing the dishes, folding laundry, making tea, or pulling weeds—in performing the numerous repetitive activities that are part of daily life with mindfulness, paying close attention to that activity and nothing else in that moment, we are fully present. Mindfulness involves adopting a particular focus toward one's experience in the present moment, an orientation that is characterized by curiosity, openness, and acceptance. Paying attention to our breathing is a simple beginning.

When we cultivate non-distracted awareness as a formal practice, we call it meditation. When we cultivate it in our home life, we call it the laundry, the kitchen, the yard.

– Karen Maezen Miller[5]

TEN TIPS FOR A MINDFUL HOME

Wake with the sun
There is no purer light than what we see when
we open our eyes first thing in the morning.

Sit
Mindfulness without meditation is just a word.

Make your bed
The state of your bed is the state of your head.
Enfold your day in dignity.

Empty your hampers
Do the laundry without resentment or commentary and
have an intimate encounter with the very fabric of your life.

Wash your bowl
Rinse away self-importance and clean up your own mess.
If you leave it undone, it will get sticky.

Set a timer
If you're distracted by the weight of what's undone, set a
kitchen timer and, like a monk in a monastery, devote yourself wholeheartedly to the task at hand until the bell rings.

Rake the leaves
Rake, weed, or sweep.
You'll never finish for good, but you'll
learn the point of pointlessness.

Eat when hungry
Align your inexhaustible desires with the one true appetite.

Let the darkness come
Set a curfew on the internet and TV and discover the natural
balance between daylight and darkness, work and rest.

Sleep when tired
Nothing more to it.

– Karen Maezen Miller[6]

To *rest* in your breath infers that you are sitting quietly and paying attention to the breath, in and out, over and over. This quiet activity is both calming and relaxing. Once we are resting in the breath, at home in the self, the capacity to be present to both ourselves and to others increases. "Resting in the breath" creates a bridge to our center. This center is sometimes called the "inner witness" or the "observing self." The practice of presence is a way to help build and strengthen this center within. We can, from this center, make clearer choices for response in each situation we encounter. The mindful attention we apply when we are practicing presence allows new insights and reflections to become foreground in our experience.

We stood together in the kitchen, the surprise of my arrival still palpable. His despair was masked by his seemingly casual attitude and insistence that "it was all good." We both knew it was not. Staying physically close, I made tea while we continued to talk. I paid close attention to his attempts to steer the conversation in other directions, gently pulling us back into the present moment. I was keenly aware of the need to stay focused on our imminent and necessary departure from his house to a more neutral place.

His attempt to end his life that morning had been thwarted by his friends, and he wanted me to leave so that he could be alone. I insisted I would not leave him until he agreed to accompany me home. I was direct and compassionate, and I did not disagree that the whole messy situation leading up to this moment was a problem. Yet I gently suggested that some of those issues might be solved and possibly re-imagined. I never took my eyes from his face, and I reminded him how much he was loved and how many people cared about him. I knew, of course, that those realities were not enough to sway his intentions in the moment, but the truth of it lodged in his heart. An hour later we left together.

It was not over, and nothing was fixed, but the momentum had slowed with the shift in energy and loving-kindness present in the room. A new road now... with some time to rest and re-think, things could emerge with time. Perhaps nothing would change enough for his desire to live to be stronger. And yet, a hope lived too: that his life could change enough to heal his broken-heartedness.

It may be that some little root of the sacred tree still lives. Nourish it then that it may leaf and bloom and fill with singing birds.

– Black Elk

 ## Exercise 2 — Practicing presence and compassionate listening

Do this with a family member or friend. Find a quiet and comfortable place to sit facing each other. Having previously practiced sitting without speaking—just listening—for five minutes each makes this exercise easier to experience. Use a timer to facilitate full and active presence.

The first speaker begins with a story of suffering, misunderstanding, hurt, or anger, with all specifics. The listener only listens, with no judgment, no emotional responses, just attentiveness—graciously witnessing. Take a long breath and a few moments of silence together before proceeding.

Now switch—without conversation—and repeat the process for five minutes. When this time is up, take a few measured minutes each—again, with only one person speaking at a time—to share how you each experienced the listening and how you each perceive the experience at the moment.

We begin this practice of mindful presence with ourselves, paying attention to the river of thoughts that inhabit the mind—and then acknowledge those thoughts and slowly begin to disentangle from them. The most common way to begin this practice is through learning to meditate. Meditation does not involve trying to change your thinking. It involves watching thought itself and eventually, with practice, entering the stillness that resides deep within each of us.

This quality of mindfulness emerges in other repetitive actions when one is paying close attention to that action. Running, swimming, singing, practicing a musical instrument, washing the dishes, raking leaves, and planting seedlings in the garden are but a few activities that induce a mindful quality of being. The meditative technique called "focusing" guides people to a "felt sense." One description of the felt sense is the subtle experience of being in a body in a particular situation—it is knowing about your life in a bodily way, listening to the body. Focusing is usually done in silence, without conversation. After such an activity we may feel more relaxed or quiet in mind and/or heart. Many athletes name this a "zone" that is elicited by a cascade of biochemical processes. Sitting still while watching your breathing, or moving in a repetitive motion, elicits this mindful quality of being.

This zone is also an energetic field. It holds a sense of resonance and a "more than" quality. This may sound mysterious and unusual, but it is very real and palpable. Something rich and clear emerges in this field. Often, an unexpected insight or depth of understanding comes to the foreground in our consciousness, where we can hold onto it and bring it alive.

The physical body is a repository of information—feelings, sensations, ideas, emotions—and focusing allows us to be at an intersection of this information. This state of bodily presence that exists before experience gets filtered into words and defined emotions is where original poetry, music, and other forms of art originate. It is the wellspring of symbols, myths, and the religious impulse. Time spent in the natural world with mindful awareness exponentially expands our vision, imagination, and creative inspiration.

 ## Exercise 3 — Cultivating mindfulness

A key element to cultivating mindfulness is learning to literally slow down and be quiet. Become more aware of your surroundings. Pay attention to what arises within you as you sit and just breathe. Become attuned to the world you live in, and pay attention to everything that draws your attention. Sit quietly and let life flow in through all your sense doors.

You can do this easily by stopping and sitting for a moment, wherever you are. This can be on a log in the woods or a sidewalk bench in the city. Breathe. Be silent. Become awake to all you notice. Slow down and rest in your breath. Be still, physically. Inner stillness follows.

What I know in my bones is that I forget to take time to remember what I know. The world is holy. We are holy. All life is holy. Daily prayers are delivered on the lips of breaking waves, the whisperings of grasses, the shimmering of leaves. We are animals, living, breathing organisms engaged not only in our own evolution but the evolution of a species that has been gifted with nascence. Nascence—to come into existence; to be born; to bring forth; the process of emerging. Even in death we are being born. And it takes time.

—Terry Tempest Williams[7]

Medicine

As dreams are the healing songs
from the wilderness
of our unconscious—
So wild animals, wild plants, wild landscapes
are the healing dreams
from the deep singing mind
of the earth.

– Dale Pendell[8]

CHAPTER THREE

Becoming Centered

Walk to the well. Turn as the earth and
moon turn, circling what they love.
Whatever circles comes from the center.

— Rumi

PRESENCE OCCURS MOST EASILY WHEN WE ARE CENTERED. This centeredness can be attained through many doorways, but the practice of meditation is the most ancient and natural entryway. Meditation and mindfulness are accessible to all who choose to learn. Being centered in the present moment is a gateway to our essential strengths and innate wisdom.

Centering is meditation in action. Within you is a space that is always calm and at peace. This space is often referred to as a "still point" or "calm center." Being centered means remaining in your calm center amidst the busyness of everyday life. Being centered means not allowing that still place within to be overshadowed by stressful circumstances or negative thoughts and emotions.

Being calm within—centered—we enter a state of clarity, focus, peace, and balance. When we are not centered, we can be unclear, unfocused, stressed, and off balance. Easy and effective centering techniques require minimal attention and focus on breath awareness. Practicing presence is a form of centering in the moment, the now. We begin again and again by focusing on the breath.

Practice presence at first for short periods of time, so that you can learn gradually what this experience feels like for you in particular. As your center becomes stronger, you will find that you can sustain your presence for longer periods of time and in more difficult situations. Eventually it becomes a capacity and habit which contributes to your health, effectiveness, enjoyment, and peace of mind.

— Tom Yeomans

Healing and transformation can be viewed as a restoration of balance. It is helpful to remember the principle of small, steady steps of continuity—so that nothing learned gets lost. This is a process that can create profound changes in a life. Practicing presence assists us in recognizing where to *move* in our lives. This can refer to a conversation or a life transition. Transformational experiences can occur over a period of time or in an instant. Practicing presence enables us to rediscover the art of truly listening, also called active listening. When we are fully present to another being, we are completely undistracted by our own inner voices, inner turmoil, or personal agenda.

Being fully present to one another takes both practice and patience with oneself. Learning to become centered in any moment increases the capacity to be fully present. Most of us are not accustomed to practicing the art of fully listening to one another. When we allow a curiousness and openness with another through listening, a softening occurs.

Practicing presence with active listening can restore an inner sense of balance. As we learn to let go of having to say or do anything, rescue, fix, or mend, and we just *listen*, we sink into the moment at hand. We do not look forward into the future or back over old business; we are fully present in the moment. Compassion becomes more possible. The word "compassion" comes from the Latin *com pati*, to "suffer with," or to "bear others' burdens with them." Here is a beautiful example of presence with compassion.

One dreary September evening there came a knock on my friend's door. She opened it to a young, scruffy-looking man she did not know. "May I help you?" she asked. He shuffled uncomfortably and then said, "I stole something from you." My friend, quite surprised, asked what he had stolen. He replied, "I took your Buddha statue." Then she remembered. It had been over six years since the experience, but it had been an upsetting moment when she noticed the statue missing from her porch one morning many years before. She had written a note and placed it where the Buddha statue had been. On it she had written "The Buddha is gone, but his spirit remains." Her clients had been upset, and one had gifted her with a replacement statue a few months later.

My friend gently asked the young man what he did with the statue. "I put it in my spare room," he replied. "I even put beads around his neck once. I did not know who it was a statue of. I used to sit there next to it. There was a fire in my apartment, and that room was the only one not touched. I decided then that I should return it to you." My friend was moved. "The statue is of Buddha. He was a great and beloved teacher, and he taught about honesty," she simply stated. The young man stared at her.

She asked him if he would like to have the statue as his own. "Really?" he stammered. "Now that you have returned it to me, I would like to offer it as a gift to you," she said. He looked at his shoes, and then up at her face. "Thank you," he replied.

My friend closed the door, and then she wept.

Peace is not just the absence of violence, but the
manifestation of human compassion.

– His Holiness the Fourteenth Dalai Lama

Through the practice of presence we rediscover the ability to actively listen. When we listen fully, and without judgment, self-reflection and insight emerge seamlessly within the spaciousness presence invokes. Natural wisdom surfaces into that expansive space. Humility, which shares its origins with the word "humus" (as in earth, or the forest floor) often washes over us in those moments. The ancient wisdom traditions call upon us to learn humility. Humility invites the false self to fall away so that the authentic self is nourished to bloom. That which falls away becomes rich compost for inner growth. Nothing learned gets lost; it becomes transformed. As we learn to respond in new ways to old situations and patterns of behavior, we become freer. This can certainly be a painstaking process, yet one with palpable results.

In order to heal, one must have the opportunity to express true feelings and speak of visions, dreams, and biography. Telling one's story—with its memories of love, loss, fear, pain, sorrow, joy, beauty, ideas, and insights—can be revelatory. It can be deeply moving in its capacity to bring light to the shadow places and understanding and clarity to the thornier aspects of relationships. Telling one's story is vital to finding the way through the dark corners of life. It is a way of revealing ourselves that can be comforting or distressing—depending upon what we choose to tell and how we choose to speak of our lives. It also depends on how we are held energetically as we are listened to. The true beauty of this elegant and simple art called presence is that both the listener and the speaker gain something. Even a small shift in perception can influence a life in myriad ways. Responsiveness grows as reactivity diminishes. Having our story—our history—listened to, without judgment, is a gift.

*What lies behind us and what lies before us are
tiny matters compared to what lies within us.*

– Ralph Waldo Emerson

Learning to be fully present to another takes practice, patience, and generosity. Discovering the inner stillness, our center, assists this practice. The experience of listening without talking back, simply being fully engaged in hearing—or being with—another is a relatively uncommon experience in today's society. We must make the choice and commitment to be present.

Many of our everyday contemporary activities become escapes from being present. Culturally, we seem a little uncomfortable with silence, alone or with company. Watching television, playing video games, mindlessly using the computer, endlessly text messaging, twittering, website "visiting," or even compulsively reading romance novels—any of these activities can become diversions from a deeper communication. There is nothing inherently wrong with these activities or distractions. Still, we must recognize their limitations if we long for more qualitative connections with others. They do not invite reflection, attentiveness, or interpersonal attunement (a focused attention on the internal world of another being). Identifying our personal distractions and recognizing them as possible obstacles to deeper communing with people, nature, and perhaps even our own inner soulfulness, is key to learning to be present in everyday experience.

To generate and increase our capacity for presence, we nurture mindful awareness. This mindfulness provides room for awareness and expansion of thought. Mindfulness cultivates stillness and a peaceful quiet within. Contemplative and reflective practices teach us how to feel comfortable with silence and quiet. This mindful attention anchors us in our lives.

"Mindfulness can be seen to involve the fullness of function in the ways that shape our sensory flow, the feelings in our minds we call affect, the nature of our thoughts, and our sense of ourselves.... Mindfulness embraces the most central aspect of how we define our mind, which is the core of our subjective life. The embodied and relational process that regulates the flow of energy and information—the mind—is exactly what mindfulness shapes. This state of being, this particular form of being aware, is all about regulating the flow of energy and information—in our bodies, and in our relationships with others."

– Daniel J. Siegal, M.D.[10]

The exciting discoveries in twenty-first century neuroscience research offer compelling information about the brain's capacity to change, grow, and heal. This "neuroplasticity" shines new light on our inherent abilities to make actual change in our bodies and minds. As mentioned earlier, meditation, silently walking in the natural world, dance, yoga, tai chi, qi gong, prayer, sitting quietly—each of these invites us into a mindful, observant attitude. They require our focused attention and lead to an inner attunement—one in which the observing self or inner witness is open, accepting, and curious about the experiencing self.

Exercise 4 — Breath awareness

While involved in whatever you are doing, bring some attention to your breathing for a few moments. It does not have to be your full attention, but just enough to bring you into your calm inner center.

Breathe naturally, or perhaps just a little more slowly and deeply than normally. After you enter a still, centered state, notice what takes you out of that centeredness. Practice taking a few deep, slow breaths each time you move out of the still, centered place. With gentle perseverance, this practice will soon bring you fully into direct experience and awareness of the present moment.

CHAPTER FOUR

Meditation

MEDITATION IS A FORM OF INNER TRAINING in which we cultivate new ways of being. In meditation, we consciously cultivate positive mental habits. We focus on a concept such as the breath, emotions, sounds, or visualized images to gain a centered state of calmness, relaxation, concentration, loving-kindness, and insight. The practice of meditation has been shown in numerous clinical studies to have many medical and psychological benefits, including promoting a sense of well-being, boosting the immune system, lowering blood pressure, alleviating mild to moderate anxiety and depression, enhancing memory and attention, and increasing alertness.

> *Meditation comes alive through a growing capacity to release our habitual entanglement in the stories and plans, conflicts and worries that make up the small sense of self, and to rest in awareness. In meditation we do this simply by acknowledging the moment-to-moment changing conditions—the pleasure and pain, the praise and blame, the litany of ideas and expectations that arise. Without identifying with them, we can rest in the awareness itself, beyond conditions, and experience our natural lightness of heart. Developing this capacity to rest in awareness nourishes* samadhi *(concentration), which stabilizes and clarifies the mind, and* prajna *(wisdom), that sees things as they are.*
>
> – Jack Kornfield

The initial endeavor in meditation is to quiet the mind and enhance non-attachment and objectivity. Only when the mind has stilled its perpetual ruminating and has momentarily abandoned its fascination for sensory experience can it readily become aware of the unconscious feelings and motivations that shape our thoughts, speech, and behavior. In meditation, one is intentionally paying attention. Meditation is knowingly directing your awareness—wise attention—to shift your state of consciousness.

Meditation is a valuable tool for finding a peaceful state of relaxation and stress relief anywhere and anytime. This sounds easy, does it not? Put your expectations aside, and don't worry about doing it right. There are infinite possibilities and no fixed criteria for determining correct meditation. Reading about meditation is like reading about swimming; only by getting into the water does the aspiring swimmer begin to progress. Begin to practice meditation by paying attention to your breath for five minutes at first, gradually increasing that time to fifteen minutes or more. Mindfulness meditation includes sitting up straight, with dignity ("we take our seat"), closing your eyes, and "watching" the breath quietly, in stillness. Ringing a singing bowl or chime to begin the meditation elicits a natural movement inward. Sound shifts our attention and awareness and wakes us up. Sound is one of the most ancient pathways to altered states of consciousness.

Meditation is not about forcing the mind to be quiet; it is about finding the quiet that is already there. Meditation helps the mind to relax into its most natural state of tranquility, openness, and simplicity, a place of deep rest and replenishment. In that relaxed state, we can be more attentive and attuned to self and others. Once we have learned how to focus on our breath, we are on the path to learning how to meditate. This does not mean that the mind stops thinking or that thoughts recede into the distance—at first. The *quiet* is in the action of watching the breath itself, in silence and with awareness. Learning to watch the thoughts and yet not get caught in thinking *about* them is the revelation. It becomes a very restful experience. We must be patient with ourselves. This is, indeed, a "practice."

Many people have forgotten that we are all capable of slowing down the constant thinking processes of our minds. One principle of Buddhist psychology states: "Thoughts are often one-sided and untrue. Learn to be mindful of thought instead of being lost in it." Noticing the content of our most repetitive thoughts offers us the chance to change and transform that thinking. Mindfulness, meditation, and meditative, contemplative actions create a spaciousness within us. Through developing a keen awareness of our thoughts and thought patterns, we begin to see how our beliefs and fears (especially in those recurring thought patterns) can blind us and keep our minds closed to other views and personal revelations. The thirteenth-century Sufi mystic and poet Rumi reflects this beautifully in the following poem.

The Guest House

This being human is a guest house.
Every morning a new arrival.

A joy, a depression, a meanness,
some momentary awareness comes
as an unexpected visitor.

Welcome and entertain them all!
Even if they're a crowd of sorrows,
who violently sweep your house
empty of its furniture,
still, treat each guest honorably,
He may be clearing you out
for some new delight.

The dark thought, the shame, the malice,
meet them at the door laughing,
and invite them in.

Be grateful for whoever comes,
because each has been sent
as a guide from the beyond.

— Rumi[12]

People who have learned how to live in such a way that they are not spending most of their time in repetitive thinking find there is room for unprecedented and surprising sensations to emerge, including an inner peacefulness. Being in the vicinity of these people often *feels* spacious. Individuals experiencing inner peace radiate that peace into their environment. As we become more mindful in daily life, it becomes easier to identify what we are feeling and sensing in the moment.

Spiritual leader, peace activist, and dedicated teacher and writer Thich Nhat Hanh teaches us that feelings can be transformed with mindfulness and meditation. In his book *Peace Is Every Step*, he describes mindfulness as a pathway to transforming difficult emotional states. He suggests that if we recognize each feeling as it arises, become one with the feeling ("Hello, Fear. How are you today?") and invite both aspects of ourselves—in this case, mindfulness and fear—to stand side by side, nourishing our mindfulness with conscious breathing to keep it alive and strong, it is possible to transmute that fear. Calming the feeling by paying attention to it, as a mother calms her baby by holding it with attention, and then releasing the feeling, letting it go while the mindfulness remains, is the key. This is a wonderful example of holding a *both/and* perspective.

Thich Nhat Hanh wisely reminds us that calming and releasing are just medicine for the symptoms, yet they make room for exploring and transforming the source of the feeling—in this case, fear. He instructs us to "look deeply." Discovering which kinds of ideas and beliefs have led to this suffering is an essential part of this process. He states, "Belief systems and firmly held viewpoints that can cause inaccurate perceptions are often at the root of difficult feelings. As we begin to understand the causes and nature of our feelings, they begin to transform themselves."

The art of living is neither careless drifting on the one hand nor fearful clinging on the other. It consists in being sensitive to each moment, in regarding it as utterly new and unique, in having the mind open and wholly receptive.

— Alan Watts

 Exercise 5 — Practicing when angry

When anger arises, walking meditation can be very helpful. Try reciting this verse as you walk:

Breathing in, I know that anger is in me.

Breathing out, I know this feeling is unpleasant.

And then, after a while:

Breathing in, I feel calm.

Breathing out, I am not strong enough to take care of this anger.

Until you are calm enough to look directly at the anger, just enjoy your breathing, your walking, and the beauties of the outdoors. After a while, the anger will subside, and you will feel strong enough to look directly at it, to try to understand its causes, and to begin the work of transforming it.[13]

When we learn to sit quietly and pay attention to our breath, we slowly become aware of the little gaps *between* thoughts. Buddhist teacher and writer Jack Kornfield names these gaps "the space of awareness within which thoughts arise." The more we practice, the longer the spaces between thoughts become. Noticing those thoughts—without judgment, just observing— and then returning to watching the breath, over and over, is a meditative mindfulness practice. It is simple but not easy, for it requires commitment and effort to apply.

Yet, it is liberating too. We begin to notice emotions and feelings that are often fleeting, yet influence our behaviors. With practice, we begin to be able to note these feelings and thoughts, yet not be attached to them. We can learn to witness the river of our conscious and sometimes unconscious inner life. We may encounter deeper emotions such as grief, anger, or fear that we might not usually allow ourselves to hold in awareness or express consciously. Also, once we have the experience of witnessing or observing the thoughts and emotions that are shaping our existence, we can more consciously choose whether or not we want those particular thoughts, emotions, or feelings to influence or even control our everyday lives. Meditation and mindful awareness allow us to more easily appreciate a full breadth of feelings including joy, peace, love, interest, amusement, delight, or happiness. These emotions often go by fleetingly and unacknowledged when we get lost in the turmoil of everyday life.

Jon Kabat-Zinn reminds us that paying attention in this way is empowering, for it opens channels to deep reservoirs of creativity, intelligence, clarity, determination, choice, and wisdom within us. He describes another way of looking at the meditation process: He invites us to view the process of thinking itself as a waterfall, a continual cascade of thought. In cultivating mindfulness through meditative awareness we go *behind* or *beyond* our thinking, like going to a vantage point in a cave behind a waterfall. We still see and hear the torrent, but we are out of the torrent. This watching of our thoughts begins to allow us space to notice our relationship to them. We become attuned to the workings of the inner self. Thoughts are just thoughts; they are not us. Thoughts come and go, rising and falling away with each moment. They are but one aspect of our humanness, among many others.

Meditating with breath awareness leads us into the inner stillness where peace and calm quiet reside.

The cacophony of sounds in the hospital room felt deafening. My friend sat there watching her dearest love, unconscious, breathing, in and out, in and out. Holding her hand and focusing on their deep heart connection, she closed her eyes and breathed in concert with her beloved, minute by minute, hour after hour, surrounding her with love. It was all and everything she could do.

Weeks later, while recounting those days together in the hospital, my friend spoke of those long hours. Her partner wept silently in gratitude, speaking softly that she never knew what was happening while she was moving in and out of her deep, semiconscious state. "It was what I knew I must do in the midst of the noise and constant commotion!" my friend replied. The felt sense of her presence and love had cocooned them both.

Peace does not mean to be in a place where there is no noise, trouble, or hard work. It means to be in the midst of those things and still be calm in your heart.

Mindfulness meditation involves sitting up straight, following the breath, and letting thoughts come and go, without trying to direct or control them. Gently bringing our attention back to the breath, over and over, helps to keep from getting lost in any confusion or chaos of thoughts or emotions without identifying with them. We learn to "keep our seat" and slowly get glimpses of another way of being. We begin to tap into a deeper, wider awareness.

Meditation provides an opportunity to directly experience how we keep trying to manufacture and hold onto a fixed identity as a defense against the uncertainties surrounding our lives.

– John Welwood[14]

Learning to meditate and focus is necessary for rediscovering the inner wisdom we each hold. As we practice more and achieve the quiet stillness that emerges from contemplative practices, a shift in perception develops. We begin to understand that our external behaviors can be supported by, and connected to, our inner guidance. As silence reflects back to us our own inner states, without interpretations or projections, the experience can feel reverential. The silence allows us the fullest freedom to be who and what we truly are; our authentic self peeks out. Silence does not interfere with anyone or anything. It leads us back to ourself.

 Exercise 6 — Beginning meditation

Find a quiet, calm place and sit in a chair, on the bed, or on the floor—anywhere that's comfortable. It is not necessary to sit cross-legged. Eliminate as much noise and as many potential distractions as possible. Don't worry about those things that you cannot control.

Sit comfortably, with your spine reasonably straight. This allows the energy to flow freely up the spine, which is an important aspect of meditation. Leaning against a chair back, wall, or headboard is perfectly all right. If, for physical reasons, you can't sit up, lie flat on your back. Place your hands in any position that is comfortable.

Focus on your breathing, slow and steady. Your central goal is maintaining a calm, non-judging awareness, allowing thoughts and feelings to come and go without getting enmeshed in them. This calm, accepting, spacious awareness is presence. Practice in this way for five to ten minutes when beginning, working up to fifteen to twenty minutes, twice a day whenever possible. You will soon discover the ease with which you enter that calm, still place within and also that it is possible to get to that calm, inner state of being in a noisy or crowded place. Breathe.

Only Breath

Not Christian or Jew or Muslim, not Hindu,
Buddhist, sufi, or zen. Not any religion

or cultural system. I am not from the East
or the West, not out of the ocean or up

from the ground, not natural or ethereal, not
composed of elements at all. I do not exist,

am not an entity in this world or the next,
did not descend from Adam and Eve or any

origin story. My place is placeless, a trace
of the traceless. Neither body or soul.

I belong to the beloved, have seen the two
worlds as one and that one call to and know,

first, last, outer, inner, only that
breath breathing human being.

– Rumi[15]

CHAPTER FIVE

Resonance

THE *NEW OXFORD AMERICAN DICTIONARY* DEFINES RESONANCE thus: "In physics, the reinforcement or prolongation of a sound by reflection from a surface or by the synchronous vibration of a neighboring object."[16] Both sitting meditation and contemplative practices invite an embodied presence that synchronizes the body and mind in the present moment. This is especially true when chanting or repeating a mantra. The awareness that emerges often includes a larger sense of environment or context than we can usually access, a *"more than"* experience. When the body and mind stop going in different directions and relax into that larger space, also called a "field," we can tap into the greatest potential of the situation. This field, which seems to feature a larger spaciousness and awareness, promotes resonance and attunement. This field is a space of transformational experiences and, ultimately, healing. Practicing presence coheres this field.

The understanding of energy fields and subtle energies and their effects on humans has been slowly making its way toward modern-day legitimacy. For thousands of years, certain doctrines and healing practices have maintained that a vital, animating force—an energy field—forms the foundation of all sentient (and even nonsentient) life. Long associated with Eastern esotericism and healing practices such as acupuncture, we are beginning to see an impact of these ancient ideas regarding energy and vibrational forces more discussed, understood, and accepted as reality. Pioneering research in the fields of contemporary medicine, quantum physics, mind-matter interactions, neuropsychology, and the emerging arenas of energy medicine and energy psychology reflect this ancient knowledge more and more.

Venn diagrams illustrate the space where things overlap, a "liminal space." This liminal space is a threshold, thought to be a place full of new information. When we are completely engaged and fully present with another, this liminal space—a *"more than"* place— is engaged. This liminal space is similar to the container or field that emerges when presence is actively practiced. In deep therapeutic work, a therapist is often conscious that a liminal space, or energetic container, is building. This place creates safety and an invitation to speak the truth. Something new and precious arrives in that space.

A few years ago, I heard the author Anne Fadiman speak of her personal experiences while writing her seminal book, *The Spirit Catches You and You Fall Down.* During her talk Fadiman spoke of the recognition that she was experiencing the edges in the lives of her subjects, and also in her own life, while researching and writing her book. This led to unexpected discoveries and illumination. The edges, or liminal spaces in life, can reveal vital information. This idea struck a chord in me, for I too have often lived on the "edges" of life. I have had important and life-altering experiences in liminal spaces and during transitional times, when it seemed that nothing was certain or constant in life.

This liminal space is also the energetic field that is often created when two or more people practice being fully present with each other. In this field of resonance that emerges, it feels as if time slows down. Clarity, expansiveness, and a sense of restfulness or relaxation are qualities of this spaciousness. This dimension of openness and s p a c i o u s n e s s may feel universal or eternal. Patterns and principles of connection, creativity, cooperation, and interdependence stir in this field of resonance.

When this occurs, an energetic shift and a palpable spaciousness seem to surround and envelop us. A richness emerges. Surprising or unexpected insights, discoveries, and often a new clarity come into those moments. These are aspects of that container or field. The coherence of the field invites a convergence of information and previously hidden knowledge. This experience can occur between two people—even if only one person is actively practicing presence—and also among groups of people, particularly when they are actively practicing presence. It may also occur in the natural world with other beings. The following event occurred last year and is seated in my heart.

It was a mild autumn night, with clouds moving in on a soft wind. I was a mile or so from home, driving watchfully, when a large, white bird glanced off my windshield and bounced off into the darkness. I immediately knew it had been an owl, and I turned my car around in the next driveway to go back to it. I saw something lying in the road. I parked by the side of the road. I stepped out to find a beautiful white owl lying on his back. I slowly walked around to his head, and I knelt down to greet him and send him healing energy. I was fully present and wrapped us both in a calm, relaxed energy state. The bird was still breathing. I was very grateful and reassured to see the soft movement of his chest.

I spoke softly, telling him everything was all right and that I was there to help him, that he did not need to be afraid. He was breathtakingly gorgeous. I hoped that he was only stunned and perhaps in shock, without serious injury. I prayed. I invited his spirit guides and mine to help us. I told him I would not leave him. I "held" him energetically, and after some minutes he opened his eyes and looked directly into mine. I smiled and breathed a sigh of relief. If only his wings were all right, I thought. I continued to speak softly, soothingly, to him. A few cars drove past, and the wind they created ruffled his feathers, lifting his wing a bit in the air flow. Time had stopped, and we were in a liminal space. Just that afternoon I had been writing about liminal space, trying to articulate that ineffable mysterious spaciousness, as it is so palpable when we are fully present with each other. A few hours later, here I was, having this extraordinary experience with a wonderful wild creature.

I stayed focused on the owl while the healer in me was simultaneously making alternate plans in case he could not stand or fly. I could get the blanket I always keep in my car and gently wrap him in that to transport him. I knew that would be frightening for him, though. I saw him try to move his wing, so I encouraged him to go slowly but keep trying. He did, and soon he pushed himself over with his wing and stood up. It was an exciting moment.

Standing there in the road, illuminated beautifully by the car's headlights, he stared directly into my eyes. He stood about four feet in front of me. We looked into each other's eyes for a long time. He never turned his head. I spoke gently to him still, telling him how beautiful and strong he was and that he seemed well and could fly off when he was ready. Time seemed to stand still. After a while, another car went by. The owl looked at me and then spread his wings and flew across the road into the trees. I felt my heart beating, soaring. I was filled with joy. I felt as if I too flew with him into the trees, and I laughed out loud with the delight of that moment. I looked at my watch as I got into my car and saw that almost twenty minutes had passed since I had returned to the owl.

Later that evening I wrote down this experience. I knew that the consciousness shift I had experienced was a distinctive moment, but the presence I felt with this magnificent owl that night was a shared ex-perience. We had been totally focused on each other, and that liminal transformational space we entered was rich with vitality. I was, indeed, transformed.

Exercise 7 — Sensing the world

Take a walk to a place outdoors where you can sit quietly by yourself. This can be anywhere in the natural world— woods, river, field, ocean, mountain, or any green space—even on a bench in the park near your job! Close your eyes, practice mindful breathing, slowing down the breath consciously, and notice what transpires. Allow your senses of touch, hearing, and smell to expand. Let the air and sounds wash over you. Practice for at least five minutes, gradually expanding to fifteen. Eventually, you can practice this with your eyes open.

Notice how you feel. How is your sense of calmness? Is there an increase in sensation and awareness of the sounds of the world? Allow the natural world to flow into your being. Be nourished. Our aliveness can quicken in the natural world.

As we become attentive to our own pulsing, breathing bodies we begin to discern our primary layer of direct sense experience—synaesthesia—the overlapping and blending of senses. This intertwining of sensory modalities invites precognitive sensations. Preconceptual and precognitive experiences of the speaking body readily transpose qualities from one sensory domain into another.
– David Abram[17]

The Venn diagram below speaks to the transcendent nature of the shared space that emerges when practicing the art of presence. It describes the relationship beween two or more entities that may have some (but not all) elements in common.

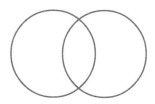

The circles symbolize interacting but complementary oppo-sites. The space within the overlap is the place in which we are called to remain, the "liminal space." This is the place where we find ourselves after we leave one room and yet have not entered another, a threshold. It is said that transformations take place in liminal spaces. Standing in that middle place is not a stance of mediocrity, but at the center and meeting point, where opposites are held together. It is a place of transformation and renewal, where authentic change begins. Inclusivity and bridging gaps are experienced in the liminal space where people meet and truly lis-ten. This space is presence experienced as a field or container.

This clarity and spacious expansiveness are addressed beauti-fully in many of the teachings of the theories and ideas of the twentieth-century psychiatrist J. L. Moreno and his work, named Psychodrama. The idea of the *encounter* in classical Psychodrama is represented by this symbol:

Moreno developed a system of action exercises, instruments, practices, and tools with which clients experience a "more than" quality and where transformational insights and new under-standing transpire. He named that space in the symbol where new information was revealed the "encounter"— another symbol of liminal space.

Practicing presence, we consciously create this field of reso-nance and a liminal space. As we move into deeper awareness and attunement together and put all of our attention into listen-ing, the words spoken into that space can re-sound with new meaning and clarity. These words, thoughts, visions, and ideas are often amplified and transmuted in that spaciousness.

Resonance as a musical metaphor is a useful and powerful image. When we practice listening with presence, we become a hearing witness—not judge, comparer, or analyst. This function of resonance speaks to vibrations and movement. We become tuning forks for each other. We resonate and re-sound to each others' voices and also to our bodies' electromagnetic vibrations. Listening with presence creates a new, resonant space that we occupy together.

Sound and singing are releases and also artistic forms that unleash and unblock resistances. Traditionally, chanting was sung in an archaic language so that it took us beyond the sound of meaning into the sound itself. Community was sustained with sound: singing and chanting. People worked together while singing. The resonance felt as groups of people chant and sing together is a physically palpable sensation. It creates spontaneous harmony and meaningful connections.

Fritjof Capra, a physicist, systems theorist, and a founding director of the Center for Ecoliteracy, suggests that biological systems are networks of chemical reactions, and social systems are networks of communications. I further propose that practicing presence affects biological systems, and subsequently, the communication among social systems.

Evolutionary biologists have recently discovered evidence that culture may have been interacting with genes to shape human evolution. They suggest that within the society populated by archaic humans, culture changed very slowly, yet among behaviorally modern humans (i.e., within the last 50,000 years), the tempo of change has been far brisker. ("Culture" here refers to humans creating tools ranging from stone implements to modern computer science and technology.)

This raises the possibility that the rapid technological innovations we have experienced during the last hundred years, and particularly the last sixty years, may prove to us that as culture has become a force of natural selection, human evolution has been accelerating. These new discoveries have stunning implications. Many contemporary thinkers, philosophers, behavioral researchers, and neurobiologists have written about the shift in consciousness necessary for what is often described as the evolutionary leap in which we humans are currently engaged. During the early twentieth century, eminent psychiatrist and psychology theorist Dr. Carl Jung spoke of a collective unconscious that weaves people of many cultures together in unseen ways through "archetypes" and shared human stories. Joseph Campbell, an American mythologist, writer, and lecturer, illuminated that thread by researching, teaching, and writing of the myths, legends, and creation stories of indigenous peoples across the human landscape.

> *People say that what we're all seeking is a meaning for life. I don't think that's what we are really seeking. I think that what we're seeking is an experience of being alive, so that our life experiences on the purely physical plane will have resonances within our own innermost being and reality, so that we actually feel the rapture of being alive.*
>
> – Joseph Campbell[18]

As we have wondered at our shared experiences and the symbols and stories that seem to assist us to make meaning of life, the shared collective unconscious may now be accompanied with an increasingly shared collective consciousness. Through modern media, the invisible connections of cyberspace now infiltrate our world events, lives, stories, and ideas, in real time, everywhere on the planet. Perhaps the emerging collective consciousness is now at a threshold. Old dogmas and ideologies may need to morph as belief systems shift and change.

Consider philosopher, educator, herbalist, and earth poet Stephen Buhner's teachings on a new mode of cognition and heart/brain entrainment: "Living organisms, including people, exchange electromagnetic energy through contact between their fields, and this electromagnetic energy carries information in much the same way radio transmitters and receivers carry music. When people or other living organisms touch, a subtle but highly complex exchange of information occurs via their electromagnetic fields. Refined measurements reveal that there is an energy exchange between people, carried through the electromagnetic field of the heart.... Our (technological) ability to measure this electromagnetic radiation is still crude.... We know that the heart generates the strongest electromagnetic field of the body and this field becomes more coherent as consciousness shifts from the brain to the heart. This coherence significantly contributes to the informational exchange that occurs during contact between different electromagnetic fields. The more coherent the field, the more potent the informational exchange."[19]

Buhner suggests that through shifting our attention towards utilizing the heart as "an organ of perception," slowly increasing the heart/brain entrainment, we have the possibility to shift our analytically taught mode of cognition that locates our consciousness in the brain and not the heart. Therefore, heart-focused techniques must be practiced to assist in the heart/brain entrainment. Buhner's excellent book *The Secret Teachings of Plant: The Intelligence of the Heart in the Direct Perception of Nature* speaks to these concepts in depth. I believe that these techniques are also examples of presence in action.

Much like athletes' reference to "muscle memory," learning to be fully present takes time to learn and apply, yet becomes easier and more natural with practice. As we learn to listen better, without allowing preconceived notions to the foreground, we can affect our most basic—and also our most sophisticated—communication skills and, eventually, our networks of social systems. Practicing presence may affect our human physiology and subsequently the "field of resonance" or coherence that ensues when people practice being fully present with each other.

Groups of people practicing presence together to facilitate communication and invite fresh perspectives and new ideas often discover commonality of purpose and experience a shared field of resonance. The following Guidelines for Group Dialogue were developed by Tom Yeomans at his teaching center, the Concord Institute. These ideas and guidelines are difficult to practice at first—it is good to keep a lighthearted approach to them in the beginning—but they become easier with time and profound in their consistent application.

During their instruction and application in spiritual psychology training, his students are guided by these principles and practice them assiduously. The shared experience of practicing with conscious awareness, attentiveness, and presence is not easy, yet it is replete with insights and collective wisdom that make the saying "the whole is greater than the sum of its parts" ring true. Experiencing this field of resonance and the richness that emerges in the circle of communal sharing can be an insightful learning experience. Learning to interact with each other in this fashion can strongly influence our daily interactions, in both our professional and personal lives.

Practicing presence in a group setting has resounding implications for communication and problem-solving in the larger world. It can lead to increased communal health and the ability to experience and value the importance of each individual. Learning to be present, without judgment, could help to create a different social fabric, in time.

Guidelines for Group Dialogue

 From our experiments with group work within a spiritual context at the Concord Institute we have formulated the following guidelines. They support the process of group learning and integration.

Circle: *Form a circle, if possible, and work within this format. If not possible, work in the spirit of a circle—nonhierarchical, inclusive, containing.*

Slow Down: *Slow down from your habitual pace of interaction and take all the time you need to listen to yourself and others, to express, to interact.*

Breathe: *Breathe fully and rest in this rhythm of breathing as you participate in the group.*

Silence: *Tolerate, accept, and welcome silence in the group, either when called for by a group member or when it falls spontaneously.*

Truth of Experience: *Speak the truth of your experience, moment to moment and over time. This includes disagreement, negative feelings, and the experience of being disconnected—these being the hardest to express.*

Deep Listening/Presence: *Listen to each other deeply and with presence. Let go of rehearsing your response, or strategizing.*

Welcome/Appreciate Differences: *Express differences and appreciate others' differences, even if this generates conflict. Hold the differences as a creative part of the group's experience, not as something to be avoided.*

No Blame/Judgment: *Suspend judgment/blame of self and others and practice simply being with your own and/or the other person's experience.*

Hold Intensity: *At moments of intensity, hold this experience in your awareness without reacting, or trying to do anything about it. Let it live in the group and be contained within the circle.*

Welcome the Unknown: *Let the unknown of your, and others', experience simply be, rather than seeking to explain, or control, the event immediately.*

Patience: *Have patience with the workings of the group and the time it takes to grow and change, both individually and collectively.*

Enjoy the Process: *Enter into the moment-to-moment changes in experience, both individual and group, that necessarily constitute the multidimensional process of human healing, development, and creative work.*

These guidelines need to be practices consciously at first, for they work in a different direction than most group norms. However, in time, they become familiar and form a solid foundation for group work.

© The Concord Institute[20]

CHAPTER SIX

Dancing into Stillness and Silence

THIS IS A WORLD IN WHICH IT IS HARD TO FIND SILENCE. That means people are more capable than ever before of appreciating it when it is there. Deep within us exist silence and freedom. That silent still-place within each of us is the place where we are truly free. Silence can be seen as the birthplace of inspiration, of our tender emotions of compassion and empathy, and of our sense of love. Silence is perhaps the last primeval experience available to us today. Cultivating the ability to become silent through meditation, contemplative practices, and mindfulness leads us again and again into that still, quiet center. It is open, vast, and comforting. The particular series of steps we move through into meditation and mindful activities are rhythmic and soothing. They invite us to slow down and relax into ourselves.

The more subtle emotions can be drowned out by the roar of the internal dialogue. When we discover the silence and still places of the mind, we no longer have to pay attention to the random and sometimes chaotic images that trigger worry, anger, fear, and pain. We develop the ability to step outside of these emotional floods and breathe into a more relaxed state. The internal dialogue going on inside many of us controls us to a far greater degree than we imagine. Learning how to become adept at stopping the noise and chatter within creates the opportunity for that spaciousness to arrive.

> There is a way between voice and presence
> where information flows. In disciplined
> silence it opens. With wandering
> talk it closes.
>
> – Rumi

Thoughts come and go. Our sense of self is not in the contents of those thoughts we become conditioned to think. As we learn how to observe those thoughts coming and going, rising and falling, we become awake to a deeper sense of an aware presence deep within us. This awareness allows room for the emergence of other ways of being and thinking. Behind the screen of our internal dialogue is something entirely different: the silence of a mind that is not imprisoned by the past.

Meditation and practicing of the art of presence invite us to pay attention to the present moment, where nothing is forced. As we softly follow the breath in and out, we slowly and gently sink into a state of relaxation and a quieter mind. We lose track of time. Here we become connected to our inner nature. We achieve a pure state of awareness that is refreshing and soothing to the mind. It becomes increasingly easier not to cling to old thought patterns. Rigid patterns of thinking and feeling begin to fall away. Moments of clarity expand. Moving the mind out of activity into silence brings us home to the self. Meditation is a kind of letting go, allowing ourselves to simply be. This is a spacious, silent, and peaceful place. Resting in our breath, we can continue to move (within and into the heart) without leaving home. Karla Bonoff, soulful vocalist and musician, sings these lyrics from her beautiful song "Home." These few lines speak to the idea.

And home sings me of sweet things
Where life there has its own wings.
Fly over the mountain, though
I'm standing still.

– Karla Bonoff

The name of her song also brings the opportunity to create more peace and spaciousness in our home by the practice of presence in our families.

The experience of being truly and fully listened to is a healing form in and of itself. To be welcomed and held emotionally and energetically by another person in that way is an astonishingly revelatory experience. As we fully express our authentic ideas, feelings, concerns, musings, dilemmas, or worries, in the sanctity of the space that is offered to us when one is totally present— is "there" for us—something stirs within us. A shift of perception occurs. We actually hear and experience ourselves and the content of our articulation differently. An experience of clarity often emerges from these moments, one unlike any other that we are used to experiencing in the complex hubbub of our contemporary lives. That is the gift of presence that we are capable of offering—in relationship to our children, our partners, spouses, friends, clients, and ultimately to ourselves.

I am reminded of the art of inviting teenagers to speak more openly and tell their stories. Usually asking a small question, and being quiet for a while after, creates room for more to be said. Food helps! It is always a delight to make tea and sit together. What transpires can be a gateway to learning more, sharing stories, and a sweet, comfortable ritual. These shared, repetitive experiences become an unspoken platform for a different level of communication to be fostered. Be patient. Be kind. Do not expect too much. Bearing witness is enough.

 ### Exercise 8 – Presence and communication with your children

Opportunities to be fully present with our children abound. Recognizing those when they appear is the key. For younger and older children alike, having tea and a snack together (the proverbial milk and cookies!) creates an opening for communication. Putting the kettle on as they arrive through the door and welcoming them is an invitation hard to resist.

The simple words "How was your day?" can elicit a shrug, grimace, or silence. But the act of pouring tea (or juice or milk...) and sitting together, waiting for words—not pulling them out—will often invite the expanded present moment to work its magic.

Allowing whatever comes to be, bearing witness, not offering guidance or wisdom unless asked, is the gateway for further communication. This quiet act of compassion and nurturing companionship can become an easy ritual. Time and honoring of this space between you and your child will open doors to deeper sharing.

Ritual is routine infused with mindfulness.
It is habit made holy.

– Kent Nerburn

Deepak Chopra, renowned endocrinologist and leader in the field of mind-body healing and quantum physics, stated "It is often said that we change who we are by changing our behavior; and we change our behavior by creating ritual. One of the reasons why ritual is so effective in effecting change is that it can lead to an innocent transformation—we are able to take small steps, make small shifts, in the smallest of increments, and very quickly our new world unfolds."[21] There are many opportunities for increased awareness and attention we can cultivate as parents. Small ways of engaging can have lasting impact and significance. Practice presence in those moments, and enjoy the re-enchantment of familial bonds.

Practicing presence in our everyday lives allows for shifts in perception from concentration to contemplation and back. Learning to become familiar with the observing self or inner witness, while feeling centered, increases our capacity for clarity and peacefulness. When we are centered and fully present, the details of our experience become vivid, and none are skipped

47

over. We are simply in the incredibly complex now. In this state of being we understand the full "truth of our experience," which is both healing and illuminating. It makes no difference what the experience is—positive or negative, high or low—what is important is that it is true in the moment. That truth, and our experience of that truth, is our aliveness. A luminosity emerges where emotions evolve and those details of experience become a window onto the vitality of life itself. The essential component of this process is to identify fully with that aliveness and the large, open space of awareness that accompanies it.

> *When we begin to tell stories, our imagination begins to flow out through our eyes and our ears to inhabit the breathing earth once again.... A revitalization of oral, storytelling culture entails only that we leave space in our days for an interchange with one another and with the earth that is not mediated by technology—neither by the television, nor the computer, nor even the printed page.*
>
> – David Abrams[22]

CHAPTER SEVEN

Many Paths to Healing

THE PRACTICE OF PRESENCE IN A THERAPEUTIC RELATIONSHIP can assist us in rediscovering a more authentic connection to our lives. Psychotherapy or personal counseling invites a reclaiming of the truth of our own inner wisdom. It is a unique and intentional interpersonal relationship. During times of amplified stress, bereavement, major life transitions, increased personal difficulties, or confusion, working with a trusted therapist can be useful in rediscovering meaning and healthy, beneficial directions to pursue in one's life. Transcendent liveliness and warmth are always present in us. A new perspective emerges as we recognize how we may have become disconnected from the sources of meaning and joy in our life—and discover new ways to reconnect to those sources. The field of resonance created within a healthy and meaningful therapeutic relationship, as the therapist listens deeply to her client, is a reflection of presence in action. In his wonderful book *The Healing Path*, Marc Ian Barasch reminds us that *meditation* and *medicine* come from the same root, which means "to care" and "to cure." When the healer creates a ritual space for the patient that is outside the ordinary, she transposes the patient into a realm of possibility where habitual limitations can be cut through.

Often a person who has experienced the feeling of being heard and held energetically in this way begins to hear herself differently. An experience of worthiness is elicited when we are truly listened to. When someone cares enough to listen closely to us and notices the nuances and particularity of expression and detail that we use in our unique form of expression, we feel valued and appreciated.

The modern, western dilemma of feeling the need to go to a professional to listen to us so that we might plumb depths of emotions, stories, and confusion is a new one. Surely there are times when an outside observer or witness is essential for a novel, considered, and wise viewpoint. Yet, if we could begin to practice presence more in our daily interactions with each other, we might begin to regard ourselves and each other with more equanimity and compassion. It seems possible that if we could begin to practice being fully present with each other on a consistent basis, the human impetus as natural storytellers would begin to assuage some of the confusion and anxiety we can feel in our present society, with its increased alienation and lack of community and coherence. When we listen well to each other, we foster tolerance and mutual respect. Appreciating our differences evolves with a deeper understanding of others' viewpoints.

One day our descendents will think it incredible that we paid so much attention to things like the amount of melanin in our skin or the shape of our eyes or our gender instead of the unique identities of each of us as complex human beings.

– Franklin Thomas

Moments of awareness and insight are abundant. Being open to recognize them when they occur is the key. A story of transition that implies much more going on beneath the surface, or a shift in perception that directs us to a previously unexplored inner knowing, can guide us to unexpected discoveries and novel solutions in our lives. When one is fully present and available to recognize these moments, and possibly mirror them back, the experience is much more conscious and concretized. It becomes accessible and relevant. The changes that may follow these types of experiences are transformative, yet they may not necessarily appear to be transformational while they are going on. These unfolding processes I am referring to as transformations are also named crises, dilemmas, junctions, breakdowns or break-throughs, and transitions. All are possible openings to growth, healing, and lasting transformation. They begin with presence and the clarity that unfolds from it.

People travel to wonder at the height of mountains, at the huge waves of the sea, at the long courses of rivers, at the vast compass of the ocean, at the circular motion of the stars; and they pass by themselves without wondering.

– Saint Augustine

Many paths can lead to healing. Contemplative practices, mindfulness, meditation, breathing techniques, and spending increased time in the natural world allow us to become more aware of our internal dialogue and dilemmas with which we may be struggling. Time spent in nature elicits reflection, perspective, and insight. Stillness and silence provide the space necessary for inner exploration. Stillness is a quality of presence. Contempla-tive practices are essential in deepening this experience of still-ness, spaciousness, inner peace, and learning to communicate with greater ease and grace.

When we practice presence, individually or in a therapeutic relationship, transformations may ensue. Healing is defined as a restoration of health or soundness. A "cure" connotes an eradi-cation or remission of the symptoms of disease or illness. "Cure" also means a return to freedom from an infecting agent. Here the word freedom represents a part of getting well again to which we must pay attention. As a person finds himself unwell, the energy or means to fully live his life are impaired. The freedom to en-gage in activities associated with normal life and a wellness state is often considerably diminished. This is a primary component in recognizing what health or healing may mean in one's life.

When illness or disease is encountered, a new—and often pro-vocative—perspective regarding one's definition of health may emerge.

Practicing presence with a person facing serious illness allows that person to become aware of the nuances and novel aspects of her particular viewpoint of living and health. Presence can support her without having to rescue or fix her. It can create a free-dom to sense the inherent mystery in a situation, free from fear. Contemplative and meditative practices that can lead to this freedom are part of the practice of presence. Vipassana or sitting meditation, walking silently and slowly while paying close atten-tion to the breath, loving-kindness meditation, tonglen medita-tion, and many other focusing contemplative practices bring us to that still, quiet center.

No Health

We put thirty spokes together and call it a wheel;
But it is on the space where there is nothing that the
usefulness of the wheel depends.
We turn clay to make a vessel;
But it is on the space where there is nothing that the
usefulness of the vessel depends.
We pierce doors and windows to make a house;
And it is on these spaces where there is nothing that the
usefulness of the house depends.
Therefore just as we take advantage of what is, we should
recognize the usefulness of what is not.

– Tao Te Ching

Redefining health is a deeply personal aspect of the healing process. When faced with a life-threatening illness, one begins to reimagine life from a completely novel perspective. Allowing a sense of freedom to be actively present in decision-making about one's personal life becomes very important—an integral part of the healing process. With or without a "cure" to an illness, ailment, or disease, there can still be beauty, love, joy, music, poetry, art, the warm embrace, intimacy, the smell of a baby, the wind against one's face, and the magnificence of a sunset. Each moment affects our sense of delight in being alive. Each of these experiences allows us to be present to the natural world, the nuances and energies of a place, and the healing moments available in situations where we may previously have forgotten to look.

For many people, facing their own demise brings about a sense of urgency regarding the priorities of people, projects, and time. Making space for the more compelling aspects of one's existence becomes most important. Being *alive* occurs with or without a cure, at least for some period of time. It is the acknowledgement of this state of aliveness—and being fully present to that state—that suggests an expansion of the definition of what health may mean as well as deeper issues of the meaning of life.

Disease, death, and serious illness in our lives present us with an opportunity to face our own impending death. Not everyone takes that opportunity for a deeper exploration. Some struggle and fight against the inevitability of death right up to the last moment of physical existence. Others take the space and time afforded—or imposed—by illness to redefine and reexamine their priorities and values, beliefs, and dreams. Holding both life and death in these moments of awareness is an immensely powerful synthesis of opposites. These intense polarities provide tremendous force. This force can seem overwhelming, and therefore it is often mitigated with other intense feelings. Fear, love, grief, joy, sorrow, anger, forgiveness, and insight are all aspects of this awareness and part of the process of growth and healing. Patience and presence are vital for moving through one emotional state to the next, allowing for perceptions to shift and sagacity to come to the foreground.

Exercise 9 – Sitting in the garden

Sit in a garden you grow, a shared green space, or in the wild—being silent in nature is the essential element. Begin with five minutes, and work up to fifteen to twenty minutes each day.

A bench or a chair in the garden provides a resting place, a space for just being in the presence of the energies of the plants, trees, and their elemental beings. This has a soothing effect and creates space for a deeper listening: to the wind and the birds who gather, to the insects and the turning of the day, and into our hearts where our innermost, quietest thoughts and feelings dwell. This presence to the kingdoms of nature presents a clearer ability to be present to the deeper aspects of ourselves. The qualities of peace, balance, partnership, and creativity become apparent as we spend more time cultivating our inner garden.

As my prayers became more attentive and inward I had less and less to say. I finally became completely silent. I started to listen—which is even further removed from speaking. I first thought that prayer entailed speaking. I then learnt that prayer is hearing, not merely being silent. That is how it is. To pray does not mean to listen to oneself speaking. Prayer involves becoming silent, and being silent, and waiting until God is heard.

– Soren Kierkegaard[23]

CHAPTER EIGHT

Expansive Experiences and
the Therapeutic Process

MY EXPERIENCE HAS BEEN THAT FOR US TO HEAL, to transform in life, we must have the opportunity to express feelings and speak our dreams and biography. Telling one's story, with its memories of fear, pain, sorrow, joy, visions, and insights can be revelatory and deeply moving in its capacity to bring light to the shadow places and understanding and clarity to the thornier aspects of relationships. Telling one's story is vital to finding the way through the dark corners of life. It is a way of revealing ourselves that can be comforting or distressing—depending upon what we choose to tell and how we choose to speak of our lives. Having someone listen fully is the fundamental component.

Myth is the history of the soul.

– William Irwin Thompson

The Swiss psychiatrist Carl Jung discovered one key to healing in a mental institution in Zurich, Switzerland. Through careful, deeply feeling observations of the imprisoned mentally ill, he realized, as one Jung biographer put it, that "every personality had a story.... Derangement happened when the story was denied." He stated, "To heal, the patient had to rediscover his story." One of Jung's great contributions was to show how we each partake, wittingly or unwittingly, in the eternal human quest for wholeness.

Author, editor, and environmental activist Marc Ian Barasch states: "Each of our life stories, no matter how mundane, is a tale of spiritual growth embraced or denied. Beneath the surfaces of everyday awareness, a larger and more inclusive self is ever pressing for realization. Ironically, even inconveniently, it is in moments of deepest crisis that this larger self may become most insistent, and our story most demanding of realization."[24]

When you are very honest with yourself and brave enough, you can express yourself fully. Whatever people might think, it is all right. Just be yourself.... That is actual practice, your actual life.

– Shunryu Suzuki

Rollo May's seminal work, *The Cry for Myth*, speaks eloquently of this healing path. His idea is that myths (in the form of storytelling) assist us with a sense of personal identity. These stories help to answer the perennial question "Who am I?" His theory that we humans need myths, even "cry for myths," as a form of interpreting our inner selves in relation to the outer world, suggests that our propensity to dramatize and re-vision our world through personal storytelling holds an enormous capacity for healing. The process is spontaneous and ongoing.

His life had been confused and discorded ... but if he could once return to a certain starting place and go over it all slowly, he could find out what that thing was.

– F. Scott Fitzgerald

It may be that this is one of the reasons that so many people who have had life-threatening illnesses often speak about the "gifts" they have received from those illnesses. As their hearts and minds become receptive to speaking about and recognizing their deepest truths—alongside their deepest fears—previously unexplored viewpoints and ideas become more welcomed. With clearer understanding, we are forever changed.

This spaciousness increases our capacity to hold the polarity between life and death. This concept describes the Buddhist practice of impermanence. Birth and death bring change. They generate feelings of impermanence. We tend to feel more comfortable with birth, therefore the Buddhist practices often focus on death. Being capable of holding both birth and death in one's consciousness—while not identifying with either—is the ultimate polarity to transcend. Practicing presence makes room for this expansive vision. It is a way to restore connection to our soulfulness. With this learning comes freedom, and also a sense of peacefulness. Everything changes.

Illness reminds us of this reality in a softer way than death perhaps, yet both create stirrings of this actuality, which allow us to hold the idea that everything changes, and that there exists an underlying oneness to the world. This principle envelops health and illness in a unifying way. It is an intuitive, holistic way of seeing the world that helps us to realize health is not something to be gained and acquired. Rather, the experience of both health and illness is a constant. It is the contrasting experiences of health and illness that allow us to gain perspective and meaning from each.

The coming together of opposites, such as birth and death, joy and sorrow, laughter and tears, or health and illness, is a theme that can be found in all cultures. The implication that opposites and boundaries are artificial and arbitrary is inherent. As presence increases the quality of our interactions, opportunities for those boundaries that are artificial and keep us from understanding each other—*seeing* each other—in a new light begin to shift and change.

An excerpt from Robert Frost's wonderful poem, "Mending Wall" speaks clearly of this:

Before I build a wall I'd ask to know
What was I walling in or walling out,
And to whom I was like to give offense.
Something there is that doesn't love a wall,
That wants it down.

Something in us, too, doesn't love divisions. We want them down. When they begin to see the interpenetration of illness and health as both aspects of a whole, like light and dark, day and night, black and white, yin and yang, ebb and flow, many people experience a huge sense of relief. Experiencing the truth of this idea creates s p a c e for other aspects of life to have meaning and importance. It assists us in developing innovative perspectives regarding how we live our lives while holding the complexity of the world.

To find some measure of peace in one's life, one must be able to identify what being centered means. Learning the art of presence assists us in finding the center, the stillness deep within, and is an important step toward rediscovering one's innermost self. This inner self can emerge only when we allow some space for it to show itself. Practicing presence creates room for this. In our busy lives, with too many commitments and too much work that extends into evenings and weekends, we need to create time to foster the sweet silence that comes from deep stillness. To cultivate the ability to find and go to that silence, that stillness, the center of oneself, takes patience and practice.

Knowing how to step back and reassess a feeling or mental state, to take a look at *what else* is occurring simultaneously with an emotion, can be highly illuminating. It also affords the observing self space to make more informed choices about how to proceed in a situation or direction in one's life. Mindful awareness of the present moment—with acceptance—is a deceptively simple way of relating to an experience that has been successfully practiced for over 2500 years to alleviate human suffering. It is based on the ancient discovery that our attempts to avoid pain and to cling to pleasure actually cause our miseries to multiply, whereas openly embracing life as it is presented, with all its difficulties, leads to a sense of ease, happiness, and an increased significance of connection to others.

Mindfulness is now the central ingredient in a number of newer, empirically supported treatments and is proving to be a remarkably powerful technique to augment virtually every form of psychotherapy. Jon Kabat-Zinn's work with people suffering from chronic pain, depression, and life-threatening illnesses has opened the door for western medicine to reconsider alternative healing modalities anew. More contemporary perspectives and techniques are taught in centers around the country and world, as the body/mind/spirit continuum continues to be explored through research studies and increasingly recognized as an integral component of healing.

Many of the contemplative arts help individuals regain balance and calm in the midst of challenging circumstances. This state of calm centeredness provides effective stress reduction and can also help address issues of meaning, values, and spirit. Contemplative practices can help people develop greater empathy and communication skills, improve focus and concentration, reduce stress, and enhance creativity. In time, with sustained commitment, they cultivate insight, wise discernment, and a loving and compassionate approach to life.

Learning how to identify—and then disidentify—from a specific emotion or feeling state affords us another perspective. This is also referred to as the cultivation of the observing self, or inner witness. Fear, which can often rule a life, is sometimes grounded in a past reality that haunts us. By becoming adept at identifying that fear, which can be mistaken for anger or shyness at times, and then faithfully practicing meditation, it is possible to gain the space in our psyche to imagine what else might be affecting us. This cultivation of that still place within creates breathing room from which we can learn to sense and discern our innermost feelings more expansively. It can also allow room in one's life to attempt to deal with a situation in a novel way. This takes courage, patience, and lots of practice. As our sense of self grows with the ability to be clearer and more discerning about our feelings and thoughts, a quiet peacefulness begins to pervade our days. Many refer to that peace as "that still place deep inside."

CHAPTER NINE

Collective Consciousness and Community

As it happens, the wall between us is very thin.
Why couldn't a cry from one of us break it down?
It would crumble easily, it would barely make a sound.

– R. M. Rilke

WE ARE ALL PART OF A COMMUNITY. This community comprises family members; friends, and often their families; co-workers and other colleagues; social, cultural, spiritual or religious group members; and the many other threads of connection that bind us in ways that support and sustain us in our daily lives. These connections may be loose or strong, frequent or infrequent, yet they each offer a sense of belonging and identity to something greater than ourselves. The person we buy a newspaper and a cup of coffee from on our way to work, the shopkeeper and check-out persons at our local stores, the letter carrier who delivers our mail each day, the healthcare professionals we see regularly, the delivery people and service workers who stream in and out of our lives on a regular basis—all these people we may not even notice consciously are each an aspect of our communal existence and a part of our community.

The future depends on what we do in the present.

– Mahatma Gandhi

While attempting to present as full a view of what assists and maintains health as possible, I suggest that we begin to become aware of our connections and interactions within the myriad communities that sustain daily life. They are each aspects of our health and well-being as clearly as the air we breathe and the food

61

we eat, the company we keep, and the songs we sing. We lack many of the ceremonies and rituals, celebrations and communal gatherings that sustained us in the many indigenous cultures and ancestral communities we evolved from. Creating new celebrations and rituals, intimate or huge, weekly or bi-annually—these will nourish connections and a shared sense of purpose.

I believe that to come back to an inner state of wholeness and health we must begin to recognize our hunger for a deeper matrix and meaning to life. When we begin to nurture our existing connections and give consideration to those, a graceful web can develop among people. Our endless willingness to share pleasantries as well as stories can enlighten and move us into a new awareness—one that tunes us into another bond, that of mutual care. Who knows? The diffusion of responsibility to each other may still be resolved.

In the beginning we attempt to cultivate loving kindness.
Later, loving kindness cultivates us.

– Stephen Levine

When we discover the ease of becoming more mindful in daily life and increasingly present to the truth of our own experiences, we slowly become aware of these links in community and observe the threads of connection we maintain on a regular basis in a natural way. We may have become removed from village life in our burgeoning towns, suburbs, and cities, but we still have almost invisible, connected webs of relationships that sustain us. Recognizing and celebrating those webs is the work, and the solution, to many conundrums we share regarding diversity and learning to live together in some peaceful way. Integrating contemplative awareness into contemporary life can help to create a more just, compassionate, reflective, and sustainable society.

What is tolerance? — it is the consequence of humanity.
We are all formed of frailty and error;
let us pardon reciprocally each other's folly —
that is the first law of nature.

– Voltaire

Practicing presence, we become more available for intelligent and compassionate consideration of each other. We notice how original, authentic, and principled most of our fellow human beings are. We all have stories, yet we lead complex lives full of information and images that do not always originate with ourselves. Opening up to a stranger by choosing to be present can amplify or illuminate a moment of life in a way that may surprise or inspire us. These opportunities exist each day within the context of our lived experience in each of our own "communities." We need only open our eyes to see them.

If we are interested in exploring a full view of what assists and maintains individual as well as communal health, we can pay closer attention to those who make up our community connections. These interactions within our communities are quiet aspects of our overall health and well-being as clearly as the air we breathe and the foods we eat, the company we keep and the songs we sing. Today many of us lack the ceremonies and rituals, celebrations and communal gatherings that have sustained the many indigenous cultures and ancestral communities from which we evolved. To come back to an inner state of wholeness and health, we must begin to recognize our hunger for a deeper matrix and meaning to life. When we begin to look after our connections, and give consideration to those, a graceful arc can develop among people, shifting the energy and quality of our local communities. Our willingness to share pleasantries as well as stories can enlighten and move us into a new awareness—one that tunes us into another bond, that of mutual care.

The idea that it has taken a few billion years for evolution to evolve enough consciousness—to become conscious of evolution—and only 150 more years to realize we can consciously evolve, is still new and startling. It is a responsibility we can and must become awake to and begin teaching our children and grand-children well how to be strong, clear and focused on helping to co-create a better world for all who follow.

— Jean Houston[25]

 ## Exercise 10 — Creating community: the potluck supper

Have a potluck dinner with your neighbors. Spontaneously invite everyone on your block, apartment floor, or scattered friends and family who barely know each other! Each person brings what they can, and it will be perfect—as shared potluck meals invariably are. Keep things simple. Music, stories, and singing may naturally emerge and can be a wonderful offering to the gathering.

As host, begin with a welcoming toast, and attempt to engage for a few minutes with each person during the evening. Listen well. Be open. Practice presence. Be kind and compassionate. Invite joy!

The great wisdom traditions, contemporary thinkers and visionaries, ancient mystics, and the rich knowledge of indigenous cultures all seem to point to the idea that waking up time is now. We are going through this chaotic evolutionary process of awakening with the possibility of an emerging collective consciousness. What might occur if we include tolerance, respect, compassion, and kindness as a standard for our next steps in evolution? The extraordinary spiritual leader of the Tibetan people, His Holiness the Fourteenth Dalai Lama, says that we achieve inner peace through the practice of compassion.

*Even our enemy is useful to us because in order to practice
compassion we need to practice tolerance, forgiveness, and
patience, the antidotes to anger.*

– His Holiness the Fourteenth Dalai Lama

The healing process is much like tending a garden. Practicing presence in our human relationships as well as in our relationships to the natural world, in both of which we are interdependently intertwined, fosters and nurtures us. The best therapeutic alliances and relationships serve to nourish us, not diminish us. We begin to feel ourselves take root in the lives we study—our own—as we recognize that spiritual and emotional development are alive and growing in an organic and complex way. Alive and interdependent cycles and spirals of life are unfolding. We may notice a pattern of growth in ourselves or our families that needs support, like a stake holding up a vine for direction. We may also become more familiar with the needs within that we are serving, those that we are not, and the deep, abiding connectedness we all share as humans in our most fundamental needs for love, bonds of friendship and community, and sustainable patterns of growth and transformation. Presence cultivates and reveals these connections.

Presence creates the condition of being free within any experience we are having and finding a joy not so vulnerable to the conditions of the "garden" within which we may be living. All gardens must be cultivated if they are to grow strong and healthy, but each one comes to maturity in its own time, and in its own way. The garden metaphor for our present human evolutionary stage has a powerful resonance. Gardens can be entered in a hundred ways and at any time. You can enter in childhood from the back door of your childhood home and continue to cultivate your garden through your entire life. Or the door can slam shut in adolescence, leaving you lost and searching for what T. S.

Eliot calls "the unknown, remembered gate." You can enter through a gate that is wide or narrow, or so overgrown with weeds that you must search carefully for the opening. You may not find your garden until adulthood or old age or the moment of death. Practicing presence opens a doorway for deeper connection and relatedness. The power of inner transformation helps to cultivate a wise and loving heart.

We humans are entering a time when our interdependence is clearer than ever. Today we understand this interdependence is no longer applicable only within our extended families and local communities, but among all humans who inhabit this blue planet and further, among all life—plants, animals, microorganisms, and the natural resources we all share.

> Out beyond ideas of wrongdoing and rightdoing,
> there is a field. I'll meet you there.
>
> —Rumi

The ability to create solutions to the environmental dilemmas we face in the twenty-first century are global initiatives today. The garden metaphor continues to inform us. As we learn to be present and mindful of the concerns in our families and communities, we also can become mindful of our connections in the larger world. A ripple effect occurs with kindness just as with fear. We can cultivate compassion and intelligent, respectful communication. These will illuminate, with presence and mindful awareness, the issues humanity faces. If we persist in learning new ways to communicate effectively and begin to experience the thought fields and energy fields we share with a sense of awe and responsibility, rather than dismissiveness and the old, repetitive thought pattern of "it has always been this way, so we cannot change it," we can evolve and grow as a species in positive and transformational ways.

Technological developments have created the possibility of a new form of human connectedness that is unprecedented. Yet, our daily interpersonal communing still weaves the tapestry in which we live out our visions, dreams, creativity, and inspiration.

Let us settle ourselves, and work and wedge our feet downward through the mud and slush of opinion, and prejudice, and tradition, and delusion, and appearance ... till we come to a hard bottom and rocks in place, which we can call reality, and say, This is, and no mistake.

– Henry David Thoreau

Have faith and trust in our common humanity. Listen better, and evolve, with a compassionate open-heartedness, and, yes, presence.

EPILOGUE

The writing of this small book has evolved as a meditation in itself for me. It represents a winnowing of my writings, thoughts, and practice about finding peace in our hearts and cultivating kindness and compassion in relationships. I have been fascinated by the intersection of perception, contemplative practices, and nervous system function for many years. I believe that social change begins within the individual. A behavioral evolution through contemplative practice can ripple outward and have expansive, synergistic effects on others. The one-on-one interactions we all experience daily are a place to begin.

The conversations encompassing the world as we know it have always included war and violence as reactions to conflict. Yet they never seem to *resolve* conflict. I envision creating conversations that *do not* include violence as an option. *The Art of Presence* is an invitation to a new kind of dialogue. Dialogue is a prerequisite for creating and sustaining authentic relationships and fostering the possibility of peace among people.

We live in exceptional times. The advent of the twenty-first century has proven difficult for many to maneuver. Its overwhelmingly fast pace, ever-evolving technological innovation, the growth of "social community" through multimedia cyberspace, global climate change, dramatic economic changes (both international and personal), and a growing fundamentalist religious fervor and anger, coupled with increasing overpopulation, have created suffering and starvation of a magnitude that is hard to grasp.

We all inhabit one world. We are all humans, and we share common stories of love and hate, joy and sorrow, family and extended relations, birth and death, making mistakes, asking for forgiveness, and hoping for redemption.

I wanted to write about presence because I believe we can learn to slow down and be still, so that we can begin to consciously re-imagine our world and have s p a c e to think about our responses. Our interconnectedness and interdependence as human beings inhabiting an evolving world that most of us have little control over is a reality we all face.

I believe that co-creating and maintaining healthy relationships stems from compassion and clear communication. During the last twenty years, I have closely followed the peace processes unfolding in Ireland, the truth and reconciliation process in South Africa, the courageous work of so many brave women and men with the refugees from the genocides in Rwanda and Bosnian rape camps and still today in the ravaged nation of Congo, and the consistent prayers for the peace process to evolve and move forward toward a restorative justice in the Middle Eastern nations. I have been keenly aware that the *art of presence* was required in each step. Discord among nations is often a reflection of discord among its people.

A deeper healing is possible only when we sense that we are truly being listened to, when we can discover the pain of forgiveness and the freedom in moving beyond our quarrel with life not being the way we might have imagined it would be. Practicing presence is an attitude, an alternative approach to meaningful communication, and the conscious cultivation of a peaceful center. Practicing presence moves us gracefully outward in our connections to others. Practicing presence is one path toward peace.

Footnotes

Cover art:

"Soul Presence Enduring" 2005 by Susan Crumpacker Murphy.

Chapter 1: Practicing Presence

1. Yeomans, Tom. 1996–1999/2002–2007. Notes from Spiritual Psychology training at the Concord Institute. All quotes from Dr. Yeomans used with permission.

2. Cohen, Leonard. Lyric from the song "Anthem" on "Live from London" album.

3. Yeomans, Tom. 1996–1999/2002–2007. Notes from Spiritual Psychology training at the Concord Institute. All quotes from Dr. Yeomans used with permission.

Chapter 2: Cultivating Mindfulness

4. Welwood, John. 1983. *Awakening the Heart*. Boston, MA: Shambhala.

5. Miller, Karen. 2010. *Shambhala Sun* (March issue) from "Hand Wash Cold: Care Instructions for an Ordinary Life." Reprinted by permission of Karen Miller.

6. Ibid.

7. Williams, Terry Tempest. 1997. "Listening Days," *Parabola* (Spring issue).

8. Pendell, Dale. 1999. From *Living With Barbarians*. Sebastapol, CA: Wild Ginger Press. Reprinted by permission of Mr. Pendell.

Chapter 3: Becoming Centered

9. Yeomans, Tom. 1996–1999/2002–2007. Notes from Spiritual Psychology training at the Concord Institute. All quotes from Dr. Yeomans used with permission.

10. Siegel, Daniel J., M.D. 2007. *The Mindful Brain: Reflection and Attunement in the Cultivation of Well-Being*. New York, NY: W. W. Norton.

Chapter 4: Meditation

11. Kornfield, Jack. 2003. "A Mind Like Sky: Wise Attention Open Awareness," *Shambhala Sun* (May issue). Reprinted by permission of Mr. Kornfield.

12. Rumi poem translated by Coleman Barks. Reprinted by permission of Mr. Barks.

13. Hanh, Thich Nhat. 1996. *The Long Road Turns to Joy: A Guide to Walking Meditation*. Berkeley, CA: Parallax Press. Reprinted by permission of Parallax Press.

14. Welwood, John. 1983. *Awakening the Heart*. Boston, MA: Shambhala.

15. Rumi poem translated by Coleman Barks. Reprinted by permission of Mr. Barks.

Chapter 5: Resonance

16. *New Oxford American Dictionary*. 2001. USA: Oxford University Press.

17. Abrams, David. 1997. *The Spell of the Sensuous*. New York, NY: First Vintage Books. Paraphrased by permission of Mr. Abrams.

18. Campbell, Joseph. 1988. *The Power of Myth*. New York, NY: Doubleday.

19. Buhner, Stephen. 2004. *The Secret Teachings of Plants; The Intelligence of the Heart in the Direct Perception of Nature*. Rochester, VT: Bear & Company.

20. Yeomans, Tom. 1996–1999/2002–2007. Guidelines for Group Dialogue. Created at the Concord Institute. All quotes from Dr. Yeomans used with permission.

Chapter 6: Dancing into Stillness and Silence

21. Chopra, Deepak. 2010. *Namaste Journal* (January issue). www.chopra.com/namaste/Jan09

22. David Abrams. 2005. " Storytelling and Wonder: on the rejuvenation of oral culture." Alliance for Wild Ethics. An early version of this essay was published in *Resurgence*, issue 222, and another in the *Encyclopedia of Religion and Nature*, Taylor and Kaplan, ed., published by *Continuum*.

Chapter 7: Many Paths to Healing

23. *Kierkegaard, Soren*. http://www.thehermitagecottage.com/heritage.htm

Chapter 8: Expansive Experiences and the Therapeutic Process

24. Barasch, Marc Ian. 1995. *The Healing Path*. New York, NY: Penguin Books.

Chapter 9: Collective Consciousness and Community

25. Houston, Jean. 2010. "The Emerging New Story," *Kosmos* (fall/winter 2009 issue).

Credits

I am deeply grateful to Susan Crumpacker Murphy, the cover artist, for her permission to use her original painting "Soul Presence Enduring" (2005). I am also very grateful to the many authors who graciously gave me permission to reprint excerpts from their published works. Their generous support and encouragement was a true delight to a new writer.

"Birdwings" by Jalal al-Din Rumi, reprinted by permission of Mr. Coleman Barks. From Barks, Coleman. 1987. *Rumi: We Are Three*. Athens, GA: Maypop Books.

"Only Breath" by Jalal al-Din Rumi , reprinted with permission of Mr. Coleman Barks. From Barks, Coleman. 1995. *The Essential Rumi*. New York, NY. HarperCollins.

Abram, David. 1996. *The Spell of the Sensuous*. New York, NY: Vintage Books.

Barasch, Marc Ian. 1995. *The Healing Path*. New York, NY. Penguin Books.

Barks, Coleman. 1987. *Rumi: We Are Three*. Athens, Georgia: Maypop Books.

Buhner, Stephen. 2002. *The Lost Language of Plants*. White River Junction, VT: Chelsea Green.

Chödrön, Pema. 1997. *When Things Fall Apart*. Boston, MA: Shambhala Publications.

Houston, Jean. 2010. "The Emerging New Story." *Kosmos*, winter issue, p. 67.

Kornfield, Jack. 2003. "A Mind Like Sky: Wise Attention Open Awareness." *Shambhala Sun,* May issue. Reprinted by permission of Jack Kornfield and *Shambhala Sun* magazine.

May, Rollo. 1991. *The Cry for Myth*. New York, NY: W.W. Norton & Company, Ltd.

Miller, Karen. 2010. "Ten Tips for a Mindful Home." *Shambhala Sun*, March issue. Also see her new book, *hand wash cold: care instructions for an ordinary life.*

Nhat Hanh, Thich. Reprinted from *The Long Road Turns to Joy: A Guide to Walking Meditation*. Parallax Press, Berkeley, California.

Siegel, Daniel J. 2007. *The Mindful Brain: Reflection and Attunement in the Cultivation of Well-Being*, New York, NY: W. W. Norton.

The New Oxford American Dictionary. 2001. USA: Oxford University Press.

Yeomans, Thomas. 1995. *Guidelines for Group Dialogue*. Colrain, MA: Concord Institute.

Reflections

Reflections

Reflections

The Author

JOANNE O'NEIL, M.A. is a psychotherapist, clinical herbalist, and author. She believes in the importance of ministering to the whole person with deep presence and reverence. Joanne practices in Montague, Newton Center, and Northampton, Massachusetts. Her website is www.moonrisemedicinals.com.